Cooking
SCHOOL

Italian Food

SARA GILBERT

CREATIVE EDUCATION & CREATIVE PAPERBACKS

Published by Creative Education and Creative Paperbacks
P.O. Box 227, Mankato, Minnesota 56002 • Creative Education
and Creative Paperbacks are imprints of The Creative Company
www.thecreativecompany.us

Design and production by Christine Vanderbeek
Printed in the United States of America

Photographs by Alamy (Bon Appetit), Corbis (68/Fabio
Bianchini/Ocean, 145/Rob MacDougall/Ocean), Getty Images
(burwellphotography, Juanmonino), iStockphoto (naelnabil,
svariophoto, VvoeVale), Shutterstock (area381, Dionisvera,
Rob Hanier, Isantilli, Vitaly Korovin, manulito, NEGOVURA,
Noraluca013, pogonici, Samot, svry, Evlakhov Valeriy,
VolkOFF-ZS-BP, Yganko), SuperStock (Cubo Images,
FoodCollection, BRETT STEVENS/Cultura Limited)

Library of Congress Cataloging-in-Publication Data
Gilbert, Sara. • Italian food / by Sara Gilbert. • p. cm. — (Cooking school) • *Summary*: An elementary introduction to the rela-
tionship between cooking and Italian culture, the effect of local
agriculture on the diets of different regions, common dishes
such as pasta, and recipe instructions.
Includes bibliographical refer-
ences and index. • ISBN 978-1-
60818-503-0 (*hardcover*)
ISBN 978-1-62832-097-8
(*pbk*) • 1. Cooking, Italian—
Juvenile literature. 2. Food—Italy
—Juvenile literature. I. Title.
TX723.G4775 2015
641.5945—dc23   2014002298

CCSS: RI.1.1, 2, 3, 5, 6, 7; RI.2.1,
2, 3, 5, 6, 7; RI.3.1, 3, 5, 7;
RF.1.1; RF.2.3, 4; RF.3.3

First Edition
9 8 7 6 5 4 3 2 1

Table of Contents

Family Cooking   4

Few Ingredients   6

Taste of Italy   8

Lots of Pasta   16

You Can Cook!   19

Glossary   24

Read More   24

Websites   24

Index   24

Family Cooking

People cook all around the world. They cook because they need to eat. They also cook because it's fun to make *nutritious* food that tastes good. In Italy, people use family *recipes* to cook tasty meals.

Italian cooking is famous for its colorful, tasty dishes.

Few Ingredients

Many Italian recipes use only a few *ingredients*. The ingredients depend on where people live, but many use *pasta* in their meals.

Italian cooks often use fresh pasta, tomatoes, and cheese.

Taste of Italy

Northern Italy is known for rich sauces made with butter and cream. It is also where Parmesan cheese is made.

Pasta carbonara (right) includes Parmesan cheese and bacon.

Tuscany is in central Italy. Cooks there make thick steaks and hearty soups using simple ingredients.

White kidney beans can be added to Italian meat dishes or soups.

Tomatoes have grown in southern Italy since the 1500s. In the 1800s, cooks in the city of Naples started using tomatoes to make pizza.

A famous story says that the Margherita pizza was named for a queen.

On the island of Sicily, cooks use fresh vegetables like eggplant and peppers. They also eat fish such as sea bass, tuna, and swordfish.

Eggplant goes with pasta (left), while seafood can be grilled.

Lots of Pasta

Pasta is served at most Italian meals. There are many different kinds of pasta, from long spaghetti to very small pasta shapes used in soup.

stelle

penne

farfalle

creste di gallo

tagliatelle

lasagna

spaghetti

conchiglie

rotini

Pizza

is a favorite meal in Italy and around the world!

INGREDIENTS

4 English muffins

1 can pizza sauce

tomatoes

pepperoni

olives

mozzarella cheese

DIRECTIONS

1. With an adult's help, preheat the oven to 375 °F.

2. Split 4 English muffins in half and place each half cut-side up on a baking sheet. Spread a spoonful of canned pizza sauce on each.

3. Add your favorite toppings, such as fresh tomatoes, pepperoni, or olives. Then top with mozzarella cheese.

4. Bake for 10 minutes or until the cheese is melted. Enjoy!

Sausage and tortellini soup

is often served before the main meal in Italy.

INGREDIENTS

1 pound Italian sausage

8 ounces cheese tortellini

3 cans chicken broth

10 ounces frozen green beans

bread slices for serving

DIRECTIONS

1. With an adult's help, brown 1 pound fresh Italian sausage in a large saucepan.

2. Add 8 ounces cheese tortellini, 3 cans chicken broth, and a 10-ounce package of frozen green beans. Bring to a boil.

3. Cook on low heat for 10 to 12 minutes. Enjoy with a slice of bread!

Pasta dishes like

baked ziti

are served at many Italian meals.

INGREDIENTS

8 ounces ziti

16 ounces ricotta cheese

3 cups grated mozzarella cheese

1 jar spaghetti sauce

½ cup Parmesan cheese

DIRECTIONS

1. Ask an adult to help you preheat the oven to 350 °F and to bring a large pot of water to a boil. Add 8 ounces ziti to the boiling water and cook for 8 minutes, then drain.

2. Put the ziti in a large bowl and mix in 16 ounces ricotta cheese and 1½ cups *grated* mozzarella cheese.

3. Pour half a jar of spaghetti sauce in the bottom of a greased 9-by-13-inch pan. Add the ziti mixture and the rest of the spaghetti sauce. Sprinkle ½ cup Parmesan cheese and another 1½ cups mozzarella cheese over the top.

4. Bake for 20 to 30 minutes, or until the casserole bubbles on the edges. Let cool slightly before eating!

Glossary

grated cut into small shreds

ingredients any of the foods or liquids that combine to complete a recipe

nutritious healthy and good for you

pasta a type of noodle, or a dish that includes noodles

recipes sets of instructions for making a certain dish, including a list of ingredients

Read More

Blaxland, Wendy. *I Can Cook! Italian Food.* Mankato, Minn.: Smart Apple Media, 2012.

Crocker, Betty. *Betty Crocker Kids Cook!* Minneapolis: Betty Crocker, 2007.

Low, Jennifer. *Kitchen for Kids.* New York: Whitecap Books, 2010.

Websites

http://www.pbs.org/food/theme/cooking -with-kids/
Find easy recipes to try by yourself or with an adult's assistance.

http://www.foodnetwork.com/cooking -with-kids/package/index.html
Learn to cook with celebrity chefs on the website of television's Food Network.

Note: Every effort has been made to ensure that the websites listed above are suitable for children, that they have educational value, and that they contain no inappropriate material. However, because of the nature of the Internet, it is impossible to guarantee that these sites will remain active indefinitely or that their contents will not be altered.

Index

cooking *4, 11, 13, 5*

eggplant *15*

fish *15*

Parmesan cheese *8, 23*

pasta *6, 16, 21, 23*

pizza *13, 19*

recipes *4, 6, 19, 21, 23*

regions *8, 11, 13*

sauces *8*

Sicily *15*

soups *11, 16, 21*

tomatoes *13, 19*

Tuscany *11*

vegetables *15*